Travel Journal
Ireland

VPJournals

Contact Details

Name: _____

Email address: _____

Tel: _____

Address: _____

_____

_____

Important Medical Information

Blood type: _____

Medication: _____

CONTENTS

Hi, I hope you enjoy this journal. It is packed with cool stuff and recommendations for you trip to Ireland, and has plenty of space to record details of your trip.

Have fun in Ireland

Great Places to visit in Ireland

Achill Island	✓
Ballyvaughan	
Beara Peninsula	
Boyle	
Caherdaniel and Derrynane	
Blackstairs and Barrow Valley	
Co Cavan	
The Burren	
Lough Derg	
Ballyhoura Mountain Bike Trails	
Blueway	
Twelve Bens	
Ring of Kerry	

The Giant's Causeway	
Skellig Islands	
Aran Islands	
Glenveagh National Park	
Connemara National Park	
Glendalough	
Wicklow Mountains National Park	
Add your own after researching	

Cool Places to visit in Ireland with Kids

Cliffs of Moher	✓
Killarney National Park	
Lough Gur / Ballyhoura	
Kylemore Abbey	
Dingle Peninsula	
Lough Boora Parklands	
Clifden / Sky Road	
Bunratty Castle	
Phoenix Park	
Dublin Zoo	
Blarney Castle	
Fota Island Wildlife Park	

Aqua Dome	
Irish National Stud & Japanese Gardens	
Add your own after researching	

Good Places to Eat in Ireland

Chapter One	✓
Coppinger Row	
Dunne & Crescenzi	
Good World	
Pig's Ear	
Juniors	
L'Gueuleton	
The Larder	
Restaurant Patrick Guilbaud	
Silk Road Café	
Sabor Brazil	
Veda	

Bloom Brasserie	
The Vintage Kitchen	
F.X.BUCKLEY. Steakhouse	
Queen of Tarts	
Vermilion	
I monelli	
Arch Bistro	
HX46	
Bad Bobs	
Bach 16	
The Old Storehouse	
Konkan	
Ravi's Kitchen	

Best Websites to Research Further

Do some more research on the internet to plan your trip:

www.wikipedia.org/wiki/Ireland
www.ireland.com
www.irishtimes.com
www.lonelyplanet.com/ireland
www.wikitravel.org/en/Ireland
www.lookaroundireland.com
www.myirelandtour.com
www.nomadicmatt.com/travel-guides/Ireland/
www.discoverireland.ie
www.tourguides.ie

More places I want to visit on our trip

1. _____
2. _____
3. _____
4. _____
5. _____
6. _____
7. _____
8. _____
9. _____
10. _____
11. _____
12. _____
13. _____
14. _____
15. _____

Postcard List

Name:
Address:

Name:
Address:

Name:
Address:

Name:

Address:

Name:

Address:

Name:

Address:

Name:

Address:

Name:

Address:

Name:

Address:

Name:

Address:

Name:

Address:

Name:

Address:

Name:

Address:

Name:

Address:

MAIL

Packing List

✓	This Journal
	Tickets
	Passport
	Money
	Chargers
	Batteries
	Book to read
	Camera
	Tablet
	Sun glasses
	Sun cream

	Toiletries
	Water
	Watch
	Snacks
	Umbrella
	Towel
	Guide book
	Kindle
	Jacket
	Medication
	Add more below

Ireland Facts

- Kerry Way is Ireland's longest and oldest walking route

- Ireland's most scenic tourist trail, the Ring of Kerry, runs 120 miles through some of southwestern Ireland

- Killarney National park, a UNESCO World Heritage biosphere reserve, is home to the 15th century Ross Castle and a herd of wild red deer

- Ireland is called Éire in Irish. It is known for its wide expanses of lush, green fields. Its nickname is the Emerald Isle

- Irish, or Irish Gaelic is the country's first official language, however the second official language English is more commonly spoken

- Trim Castle was the first Anglo-Norman castle built (1169) in Ireland, as well as the largest ever built

- The world famous Guinness beer is from Ireland, it originated in the Dublin brewery of Arthur Guinness

- Gaelic football and hurling are traditional sports of Ireland and remain the most popular sports in the country

- At the Olympics, boxing is Ireland's most successful sport

- The River Shannon is the Longest River in Ireland

- Ireland's highest point is Carrauntoohil. But if you are fit enough, we recommend you trek up Croagh Patrick in County Mayo, this holy mountain attracts 1 million visitors each year

- The Shamrock is the national symbol of Ireland and along with the harp it is a registered trademark of the country

- Ireland is a snake-free island. Due to its isolation from the European mainland, Ireland lacks several species common elsewhere in Europe, such as moles, weasels, polecats or roe deer

- The longest place name in Ireland is Muckanaghederdauhaulia, in County Galway

- The Royal Cork Yacht Club was founded in 1720 and is the world's oldest yacht club

- The story of the world-famous vampire Count Dracula was written in 1897 by Bram Stoker, from Dublin

- Glendalough, or the 'Valley of Two Lakes', is one of Ireland's most prominent monastic sites, nestled in the heart of the Wicklow Mountains National Park.

Clothes & Shoe Sizes

Children's Shoe Sizes

UK	EUROPE	US	Japan
4	20	4½ or 5	12 ½
4 ½	21	5 or 5½	13
5	21 or 22	5½ or 6	13 ½
5 ½	22	6	13½ or 14
6	23	6½ or 7	14 or 14½
6 ½	23 or 24	7 ½	14½ or 15
7	24	7½ or 8	15
7 ½	25	8 or 9	15 ½
8	25 or 26	8½ or 9	16
8 ½	26	9½	16 ½
9	27	9½ or 10	16 ½ or 17
10	28	10½ or 11	17 ½
10½ or 11	29	11½ or 12	18
11 ½	30	12½	18 or 18 ½
12	31	13	19 or 19 ½
12 ½	31	13 or 13½	19 ½ or 20
13	32	1	20
13 ½	32 ½	1 ½	20 ½
1	33	1½ or 2	21
2	34	2½ or 3	22

Children's Clothing Sizes

UK	EUROPE	US	Australia
12m	80cm	12-18m	12m
18m	80-86cm	18-24m	18m
24m	86-92cm	23-24m	2
2-3	92-98cm	2T	3
3-4	98-104cm	4T	4
3-5	104-110cm	5	5
5-6	110-116cm	6	6
6-7	116-122cm	6X-7	7
7-8	122-128cm	7 to 8	8
8-9	128-134cm	9 to 10	9
9-10	134-140cm	10	10
10-11	140-146cm	11	11
11-12	146-152cm	14	12

Women's Shoe Sizes

UK	EUROPE	US	Japan
3	35 ½	5	22 ½
3 ½	36	5 ½	23
4	37	6	23
4 ½	37 ½	6 ½	23 ½
5	38	7	24
5 ½	39	7 ½	24
6	39 ½	8	24 ½
6 ½	40	8 ½	25
7	41	9 ½	25 ½
7 ½	41 ½	10	26
8	42	10 ½	26 ½

Women's Clothes Sizes

UK	US	Japan	France / Spain	Germany	Ireland	Australia
6/8	6	7-9	36	34	40	8
10	8	9-11	38	36	42	10
12	10	11-13	40	38	44	12
14	12	13-15	42	39	46	14
16	14	15-17	44	40	48	16
18	16	17-19	46	42	50	18
20	18	19-21	48	44	52	20

Men's Shoe Sizes

UK	EUROPE	US	Japan
6	38 ½	6 ½	24 ½
6 ½	39	7	25
7	40	7 ½	25 ½
7 ½	41	8	26
8	42	8 ½	27 ½
8 ½	43	9	27 ½
9	43 ½	9 ½	28
9 ½	44	10	28 ½
10	44	10 ½	28 ½
10 ½	44 ½	11	29
11	45	12	29 ½

Men's Suit / Coat / Sweater Sizes

UK / US / Aus	EU / Japan	General
32	42	Small
34	44	Small
36	46	Small
38	48	Medium
40	50	Large
42	52	Large
44	54	Extra Large
46	56	Extra Large

Men's Pants / Trouser Sizes (Waist)

UK / US	Europe
32	81 cm
34	86 cm
36	91 cm
38	97 cm
40	102 cm
42	107 cm

We have included another copy of this at the back of the book, so you can find it quickly again when you are in Ireland

Ireland Trip Diary

Write a daily diary during your trip

Day 1

Date: _____   **Weather:** _____

Day 2

Date: _____   **Weather:** _____

_____

_____

_____

_____

_____

_____

_____

_____

_____

_____

_____

_____

_____

_____

Day 3

Date: _____   **Weather:** _____

_____

_____

_____

_____

_____

_____

_____

_____

_____

_____

_____

_____

_____

_____

_____

_____

Day 4

Date: _____ **Weather:** _____

Day 5

Date: _____   **Weather:** _____

_____

_____

_____

_____

_____

_____

_____

_____

_____

_____

_____

_____

_____

_____

Day 6

Date: _____   **Weather:** _____

_____

_____

_____

_____

_____

_____

_____

_____

_____

_____

_____

_____

_____

_____

Day 7

Date: _____   **Weather:** _____

Day 8

Date: _____   **Weather:** _____

Day 9

Date: _____   **Weather:** _____

_____

_____

_____

_____

_____

_____

_____

_____

_____

_____

_____

_____

_____

Day 10

Date: _____   **Weather:** _____

_____

_____

_____

_____

_____

_____

_____

_____

_____

_____

_____

_____

_____

_____

Day 11

Date: _____   **Weather:** _____

Day 12

Date: _____   **Weather:** _____

_____

_____

_____

_____

_____

_____

_____

_____

_____

_____

_____

_____

_____

_____

75

Day 13

Date: _____   **Weather:** _____

Day 14

Date: _____   **Weather:** _____

_____

_____

_____

_____

_____

_____

_____

_____

_____

_____

_____

_____

_____

_____

Day 15

Date: _____   **Weather:** _____

Day 16

Date: _____   **Weather:** _____

_____

_____

_____

_____

_____

_____

_____

_____

_____

_____

_____

_____

_____

_____

Day 17

Date: _____   **Weather:** _____

Day 18

Date: _____   **Weather:** _____

Day 19

Date: _____   **Weather:** _____

_____

_____

_____

_____

_____

_____

_____

_____

_____

_____

_____

_____

_____

Day 20

Date: _____   **Weather:** _____

Day 21

Date: _____   **Weather:** _____

_____

_____

_____

_____

_____

_____

_____

_____

_____

_____

_____

_____

_____

Memories of your Trip

Things I will remember from the trip

Favorite Places visited on the Trip

People I Met

Name:
Address:
Tel:
email:

Name:
Address:
Tel:
email:

Name:
Address:
Tel:
email:

Name:
Address:
Tel:
email:

Name:
Address:
Tel:
email:

Name:
Address:
Tel:
email:

Name:
Address:
Tel:
email:

Name:	
Address:	
Tel:	
email:	

Name:	
Address:	
Tel:	
email:	

Name:	
Address:	
Tel:	
email:	

Name:	
Address:	
Tel:	
email:	

We hope you enjoyed your trip to Ireland

Please leave us a review if you found this Journal useful

Check out our useful resources on the next few pages

Clothes & Shoe Sizes

Children's Shoe Sizes

UK	EUROPE	US	Japan
4	20	4½ or 5	12 ½
4 ½	21	5 or 5½	13
5	21 or 22	5½ or 6	13 ½
5 ½	22	6	13½ or 14
6	23	6½ or 7	14 or 14½
6 ½	23 or 24	7 ½	14½ or 15
7	24	7½ or 8	15
7 ½	25	8 or 9	15 ½
8	25 or 26	8½ or 9	16
8 ½	26	9½	16 ½
9	27	9½ or 10	16 ½ or 17
10	28	10½ or 11	17 ½
10½ or 11	29	11½ or 12	18
11 ½	30	12½	18 or 18 ½
12	31	13	19 or 19 ½
12 ½	31	13 or 13½	19 ½ or 20
13	32	1	20
13 ½	32 ½	1 ½	20 ½
1	33	1½ or 2	21
2	34	2½ or 3	22

Children's Clothing Sizes

UK	EUROPE	US	Australia
12m	80cm	12-18m	12m
18m	80-86cm	18-24m	18m
24m	86-92cm	23-24m	2
2-3	92-98cm	2T	3
3-4	98-104cm	4T	4
3-5	104-110cm	5	5
5-6	110-116cm	6	6
6-7	116-122cm	6X-7	7
7-8	122-128cm	7 to 8	8
8-9	128-134cm	9 to 10	9
9-10	134-140cm	10	10
10-11	140-146cm	11	11
11-12	146-152cm	14	12

Women's Shoe Sizes

UK	EUROPE	US	Japan
3	35 ½	5	22 ½
3 ½	36	5 ½	23
4	37	6	23
4 ½	37 ½	6 ½	23 ½
5	38	7	24
5 ½	39	7 ½	24
6	39 ½	8	24 ½
6 ½	40	8 ½	25
7	41	9 ½	25 ½
7 ½	41 ½	10	26
8	42	10 ½	26 ½

Women's Clothes Sizes

UK	US	Japan	France / Spain	Germany	Ireland	Australia
6/8	6	7-9	36	34	40	8
10	8	9-11	38	36	42	10
12	10	11-13	40	38	44	12
14	12	13-15	42	39	46	14
16	14	15-17	44	40	48	16
18	16	17-19	46	42	50	18
20	18	19-21	48	44	52	20

Men's Shoe Sizes

UK	EUROPE	US	Japan
6	38 ½	6 ½	24 ½
6 ½	39	7	25
7	40	7 ½	25 ½
7 ½	41	8	26
8	42	8 ½	27 ½
8 ½	43	9	27 ½
9	43 ½	9 ½	28
9 ½	44	10	28 ½
10	44	10 ½	28 ½
10 ½	44 ½	11	29
11	45	12	29 ½

Men's Suit / Coat / Sweater Sizes

UK / US / Aus	EU / Japan	General
32	42	Small
34	44	Small
36	46	Small
38	48	Medium
40	50	Large
42	52	Large
44	54	Extra Large
46	56	Extra Large

Men's Pants / Trouser Sizes (Waist)

UK / US	Europe
32	81 cm
34	86 cm
36	91 cm
38	97 cm
40	102 cm
42	107 cm

Common Translations

English	French	Spanish	Italian
Hello	Bonjour	Hola	Ciao
Goodbye	Au revoir	Adiós	Arrivederci
Yes	Oui	Sí	Si
No	Non	No	No
Please	S'il-vous-plaît	Por favor	Per favore
Thank you	Merci	Gracias	Grazie
Excuse me	Excusez-moi	Perdón	Mi scusi
How much	Combien	Cuánto	Quanto
My name is	Mon nom est	Mi nombre es	Io mi chiamo
Where is	Où est	Dónde está	Dov'è
The bank	La banque	El banco	La banca
The toilet	Les toilettes	El baño	Il bagno

German	Japanese	Mandarin	Hindi
Hallo	Kon'nichiwa	Ni hao	Namaste
Auf Wiedersehen	Sayonara	Zaijian	Alavida
Ja	Hai	Shi de	Ham
Nein	Ie	Meiyou	Nahim
Bitte	Onegaishimasu	Qing	Krpaya
Vielen Dank	Arigato	Xiexie	Dhan'yavada
Entschuldigung	Sumimasen	Duoshao	Mujhe mapha karem
Wie viel	Ikura	Wo de mingzi shi	Kitana
Mein Name ist	Watashinonamaeha	Nali	Mera nama hai
Wo ist	Doko ni aru	Yinhang	Kaham hai
Die Bank	Ginko	Yinhang	Bainka
Die Toilette	Toire	Cesuo	Saucalaya

Notes:

Made in United States
North Haven, CT
02 October 2023

42281389R00076